Original title:
Tropical Escape

Copyright © 2025 Creative Arts Management OÜ
All rights reserved.

Author: Liam Sterling
ISBN HARDBACK: 978-1-80581-487-0
ISBN PAPERBACK: 978-1-80581-014-8
ISBN EBOOK: 978-1-80581-487-0

Paradise Awaits

In the sun, yelling 'Bingo!', I play,
With a coconut drink and a towel's ray.
My only worry? Where's my flip-flop?
In this sand castle, who's scheduling the stop?

Laughter bubbles up like a fizzy drink,
I trip on my towel, then wink and think.
The crabs on the beach all dance in a line,
Inviting me over, 'Come join our dine!'

Whispering Palms

Under the palms, I chase a breeze,
While seagulls giggle at silly trees.
With a hat made of fruit, I look quite absurd,
But a parrot flies by, and he's not disturbed.

Sunglasses on, I pretend to be cool,
Splashing at waves like a kid in a pool.
The shells on my feet, oh what a delight,
Each one a hidden treasure, oh what a sight!

Sunlit Shores

On sunlit shores, I spot a big fish,
It wriggles away, not granting my wish.
I flip-flop with grace, or maybe I just trip,
As sand sticks to my ice cream, a sugary blip.

Laughter erupts, it's salad for our lunch,
Seagull swoops in, 'Did you bring the crunch?'
With beach balls bouncing, and laughter so loud,
We form a parade, oh look at our crowd!

Journey to the Isles

Off to the isles, we pack all our dreams,
With sunscreen and snacks, what a comical team!
A boat full of giggles, and snacks on a tray,
A seagull steals chips, oh what a display!

We dance on the deck, like fools in the sun,
With wiggles and jiggles, we're all having fun.
The compass says 'North', but we're headed to 'laugh',
In search of a treasure, maybe a warm bath!

Echoes of the Ocean

Waves giggle and splash, it's a playful affair,
Jellyfish in glasses, oh what a rare pair!
Seagulls squawk jokes, with a wink and a nod,
Each fish is a clown, making fun of the cod.

Beach balls are bouncing, laughter fills the air,
A crab doing the moonwalk, without a care!
Shells harmonize tunes, as the sunset turns gold,
In this watery circus, we let our souls fold.

Serene Sunsets

The sun sinks like a pineapple, sweet and bright,
Colors clash wildly, what a silly sight!
Bananarama dancing, under the flamingo glow,
As the horizon frowns, just putting on a show.

Cocktails with umbrellas, they cheer for the moon,
The stars might just twerk, they'll be out there soon!
Palm trees are giggling, in the warm evening breeze,
Swaying to rhythms that tickle the seas.

Vibrant Hideaway

In a cove where coconuts drop on your head,
Silly monkeys mimic, you'll laugh till you're red!
Sun hats and flip-flops are the style of the day,
With feet in the sand, we'll dance and we'll sway.

A hammock is calling, with snacks on the side,
While squirrels throw coconuts, what a bumpy ride!
Palm fronds are fans, keeping everyone cool,
In this hideaway bustling, we're nobody's fool.

Embrace of the Breeze

The wind whispers secrets, with a chuckle or two,
While the leaves have a gossip, just for the crew!
Kites twist and rumble, like they're in a race,
Up high in the heavens, they're having a chase.

A picnic of laughter, with fruit-shaped balloons,
Seashells are wearing their best cartooned tunes!
Every gust brings a giggle, a tickle on skin,
In this breeze of delight, let the fun times begin!

Treasures of the Tide

A crab in shades, sunbathing wide,
Claims he's the king of the ocean tide.
With his tiny crown, he struts with flair,
But watch your toes, he doesn't care!

Seashells giggle, pearls play hide,
As the starfish dance, they try to glide.
A fish in a bow tie, what a sight!
He'll dance your socks off, try not to fright!

Voyage of the Vivid

A parrot in stripes, all dressed to impress,
Sings off-key tunes, causing quite a mess.
He tries to tango with a beach ball's bounce,
Every failed move makes the crabs pounce!

The sun wears sunglasses, quite the charade,
As it grins down on the beach parade.
Sandy toes shuffle, lost in delight,
Chasing ice cream cones, oh what a sight!

Whispers of the Palms

Coconuts chuckle as the breeze sighs,
They're up to mischief, playing disguise.
One rolls down as a kid takes a swing,
The laughter erupts, oh, what joy they bring!

Palm branches are gossiping, what a tune,
"Did you see Fred, he thinks he's a boone?"
With sunburned noses and hats askew,
They dance in circles, waving just for you!

Sun-Kissed Mornings

With pancakes flipping, seagulls in flight,
A sleepily groggy beach bum ignites.
He spills his juice, with a splash and a grin,
As the ocean chuckles, welcomes him in!

Morning glories peak under the sun,
"Let's race the tides, it'll be so much fun!"
But look out for seagulls, they're crafty and sly,
They'll snatch your toast as you wave goodbye!

Kaleidoscope of Color

A parrot in sunglasses struts on the shore,
Sand between my toes, who could ask for more?
Coconuts fall with a thud and a splash,
I dodge the fruit with an ungraceful dash.

The sun wears a smile while I sip on a drink,
Goldfish in my cocktail, making me think:
Did I just see a crab doing the cha-cha?
Or was that my cousin, zipping off to drama?

Palm trees gossip in the warm ocean breeze,
While iguanas play cards with such practiced ease.
A beach ball bounces and rolls down the sand,
Next thing I know, I'm part of the band.

As night falls, the stars put on a show,
With laughter and music, we dance to and fro.
Underneath swaying lights, we share a big grin,
Here in this paradise, let the fun begin!

Home for the Wanderer

Flip-flops flapping, I'm lost in the waves,
Chasing after seagulls, oh, how they behave!
The map says 'lost', but my heart says 'found',
In this land of laughter, joy knows no bound.

Sand castles tumble like dreams in the wind,
While I giggle and tumble, a playful rescind.
A crab waves hello as it scuttles by fast,
It seems I'm the slowpoke, the die always cast.

Sipping on fruit beverages, you'd think I'm refined,
But I just saw a hermit, with my drink, he aligned!
He pinched it right off, oh what a surprise,
Now we share the sunset, two thieves on the rise!

With every misstep, the world feels alive,
In the heart of the island, that's where I thrive.
The wanderer in me finds a home in the sun,
Chasing wild adventures, oh, this is my fun!

Serenity in Every Breeze

Swaying in the hammock, I dream of a snack,
While palm leaves rustle, they start their own crack.
The fish jump like popcorn, just waiting to fry,
And here comes the seagull, oh me, oh my!

Clouds shaped like slippers drift across the skies,
I swear I just saw one blink its big eyes.
A crab brings me treasure, a shell full of fries,
In the land of the silly, my laughter soon flies.

Is that a mirage or a giant ice cream?
The heat plays tricks, it's a whimsical dream.
I chase after rainbows, but slip in the goo,
Why is there jelly right here on my shoe?

Even the coconuts giggle in glee,
As I chase off the laughter, so wild and so free.
Every gentle breeze carries stories untold,
In this realm of the funny, I'll forever unfold!

Island Heartbeat

Dancing on sand, with no place to be,
A lobster parade, just welcoming me!
I trip over flip-flops, but hey, that's my style,
With every misstep, I wear a big smile.

The rhythm of waves plays an offbeat tune,
As I join in the chorus, beneath the bright moon.
A jellyfish waltzes, just trying to groove,
Who knew they'd be better? Now I've got to move!

A conch shell is buzzing, I ask it to speak,
It tells me a secret, but it's rather oblique.
What's life without giggles? No plan needed here,
With sea creatures partying, I have no more fear.

As the sun paints the sky in hues of delight,
I join in the madness, it feels just right.
The heartbeat of the island, wild and complete,
In this land of the funny, I've found my own beat!

Island Dreams in Sunlight Streams

On sandy shores, I've made a throne,
Where lizards dance like they're on loan.
A coconut dropped, I wear it proud,
My royal crown in the sunshine loud.

The sun is bright, like a toddler's grin,
And seagulls squawk, they want to win.
I toss some snacks, they dive with glee,
These feathered friends are wacky, you see.

With every splash, my troubles fade,
As crabs do conga on parade.
I join the fun, my moves are wild,
A sunburned king, forever a child.

So grab your flip-flops, join the scene,
Life's a beach, not so serious, I mean.
Let's laugh and play 'til the twilight hums,
In island dreams, where no one succumbs.

The Lush Green Getaway

In a hammock strung beneath the trees,
The monkeys steal my snacks with ease.
They chatter loud, as if to say,
'This is our jungle, now go away!'

Parrots squawk in colors bright,
While I try to nap in midday light.
A mosquito whispers, 'Come take a bite!'
I swat and shout, 'You're ruining my night!'

The salad's fresh, with ants in tow,
They steal my lunch without a show.
I laugh and share my meal with flair,
A feast for critters—'Bon appétit, air!'

So when you hear the jungle's song,
Join the party, it won't be long.
With laughter loud and shenanigans rife,
In this green getaway, we love our life.

Lemonade Skies at Dusk

As the sun dips low in skies of gold,
I sip on citrus, feeling bold.
The clouds are cotton candy dreams,
And laughter bubbles in warm streams.

My friend's a parrot, my partner in fun,
He squawks out jokes, we're never done.
With every wave, we dance and sway,
Who needs a plan? Let's drift away!

The sand's a comedy stage tonight,
As tourists trip in their beachy plight.
I giggle at all as I sip and munch,
Life's too short, so let's have a punch!

The stars come out to join the jest,
In this sweet twilight, we're truly blessed.
With lemonade skies, we toast our cheer,
To whimsical moments, we hold dear.

Where the Ocean Meets the Sky

At the brink of where blue waves crash,
I built a sandcastle, made in a flash.
A crab's my knight, and shells my moat,
With flip-flops lost, I'm feeling remote.

The ocean's laughter, a bubbly tune,
And jellyfish dance like balloons in June.
I wave hello, they wave back with flair,
Underwater waltz, what a funny affair!

The sun kisses waves, in a friendly tease,
While Seaweed Sally plays tag with the breeze.
I join the frolics, let my worries float,
As sea critters plan a silly boat.

In this sandy realm, nothing's too sly,
Where folly rules and worries just fly.
With playful hearts, we always try,
To laugh and twirl 'neath the ocean's sky.

Chill Vibes of the Coast

Flip-flops squeak, the sand is warm,
A seagull dances, causing alarm.
Ice cream drips down my shirt, oh dear,
The beach is a circus, full of cheer.

Lounge chairs gossip, sunburns compete,
While crabs scuttle, two-stepping their beat.
A beach ball tricks a dive from my friend,
Splashing water, laughter does not end.

Sunscreen battles with the salty breeze,
Coconuts clatter and sway from the trees.
Beach hats fly like kites in the air,
Sandy surprises, nothing can compare.

As the sun dips low, we grin and we cheer,
A day full of folly, supplies for the year.
With salty snacks and coconut drinks,
Life on the coast is just what one thinks.

A Journey to the Edge of the World

A boat full of snacks, we set out at dawn,
The captain is laughing, his compass is gone.
Waves high-five our hull, a splash and a yelp,
Not a pirate in sight, just some seaweed kelp.

Fish in tuxedos swim past with a wink,
While dolphins perform, oh what a sync!
Our map's upside down, who knows where we are?
Just throw in a line, we'll catch dinner from afar.

The horizon giggles, as gulls share a joke,
The sun throws confetti, we're laughing for smoke.
Bumpy ride ahead, hold onto your snacks,
With every big wave, there's laughter that cracks.

What treasure we find at the edge of the blue?
Is it gold? Or just more snacks for our crew?
Adventure is wild, with giggles and swells,
At the world's very end, where the fun truly dwells.

Basking in Tropical Sunlight

Sunglasses on, sipping coconut thrill,
The beach is a stage and the sun's giving chills.
Umbrellas spin stories in colors so bright,
As beachgoers groove, what a wonderful sight!

The seagulls hold court, their voices a buzz,
While flip-flop fashion becomes quite the fuzz.
A giant inflatable, it floats with great pride,
A merry parade on the waves, what a ride!

A sandcastle fortress, decorated by dreams,
With towers of seaweed and moats lined with creams.
The tide rolls in gently, we shriek with delight,
As seashells applaud in their own salty rite.

Underneath palm trees, we giggle and munch,
Crispy fried plantains, a sizzling lunch.
In the glow of the sun, with laughter so free,
We find our true fortune: just you, beach, and me.

Footprints in the Golden Dust

On a sandy beach, I tried to jog,
But tripped and fell, landing like a frog.
The sun was bright, my hat flew high,
I swatted at seagulls, gave it a try.

Footprints danced, like a silly song,
I followed them back, where I felt I belonged.
A crab waved hello, or was it a 'bye'?
I think I've made friends, oh me, oh my!

Sand sandy snacks drifted on by,
I reached for a chip, a gull dared to fly.
It swooped, it dived, stole my last bite,
Now I chase it down like I'm in a fight.

With laughter and splashes, the day rolls on,
Beach games and giggles, from dusk till dawn.
The golden dust sparkles, a comical scene,
Who knew a beach could be so serene?

The Call of the Sea

The ocean called, 'Come play with me!'
Waves and whales giggling, so wild and free.
I brought my float, what a sight to see,
But it popped like my hopes, oh woe is me!

My friend brought a boat, that tipped with glee,
We splashed and we wobbled, just like a spree.
The fish in their schools shouted, 'Look at you!'
I thought they were cool, but they swam right through.

A seagull perched high, gave me a wink,
I offered it fries, but it paused to think.
It guffawed in delight, as it took to the skies,
It seemed to enjoy my fries, oh my, oh my!

With laughter in waves, and sun on our skin,
We swam like the dolphins, oh where to begin?
In the call of the sea, we danced and we'd sway,
With smiles so bright, we hoped it wouldn't end today.

Serenity Amongst the Flora

In the jungle's embrace, I strolled with flair,
Thought I'd blend in, with my flower hair.
A monkey laughed hard, then stole my drink,
Is it a jungle or just my bad luck, I think?

The trees whispered secrets of creatures galore,
While climbing high, I tangled with vines I swore.
The flowers bobbed heads, as I tried to pass,
They giggled and jiggled, oh what a class!

Each petal a gem, in vibrant display,
I found my heart racing, didn't know it could sway.
A bright parrot swooped in, with a cackle so sweet,
It mimicked my laugh, what a hilarious feat!

Amongst the flora, chaos now blooms,
With giggles and grins, filling the rooms.
Nature's a comedian, who knew its worth?
In this serene madness, I've found my mirth!

Melodies of the Island

A ukulele strums, on a bright sunny day,
The island sings songs in a humorous way.
The coconuts chuckle from their treetop beds,
As the tourists dance silly, bumping their heads.

The sun's a cheeky fellow, making us glow,
While sunscreen promises, turn us to snow.
With splashes and laughter, joy fills the air,
While I trip on my flip-flops, like I just don't care!

A crab joined the conga, in its own little groove,
All the sea shells swayed, finding their move.
The palm trees swayed with a tropical beat,
As we spun and giggled, happy and fleet.

From sunset to twilight, the music won't cease,
With melodies swirling, imparting such peace.
Let the rhythms enchant, come dance here with me,
In this quirky paradise, so wild and free!

Driftwood Stories

On a beach with sand so bright,
A seagull stole my sandwich bite.
I chased it with a squeaky yell,
But it just sat there, feeling swell.

The waves danced in a silly tune,
While crabs joined in, a sandy boon.
They pinched my toe, I squealed in glee,
Nature's quarrels were just for me.

Old driftwood told me tales of old,
Of pirate ships and treasures gold.
I listened close, my drink in hand,
Imagining life on this wild strand.

Beneath the Mango Trees

Beneath the leaves, a party grows,
As mangoes drop—oh, what a prose!
They roll around, like playful kids,
Creating laughs, while mischief bids.

I tried to catch one flying by,
But tripped and made a funny sigh.
The squirrels chuckled, perched above,
As I cursed my fruitless love.

We danced and sang to nature's tune,
With sticky fingers, afternoon.
The sun performed its bright ballet,
As laughter colored every ray.

A Breeze in Bloom

The flowers swayed with every jest,
As bees declared a buzzing fest.
I waved my arms like I was mad,
But blossoms giggled, oh so glad.

A gentle breeze came to our side,
It tossed my hat—a wild ride!
I chased it down, through sun and shade,
While flowers joined the grand charade.

Their petals whispered silly things,
About the joy that laughter brings.
In this paradise, faint and neat,
Each breath was filled with fun's heartbeat.

Starlit Nights on Warm Sand

Under the stars, the moonlight's play,
I built a castle, come what may.
A crab moved in—claimed it for his own,
His tiny throne, a regal zone.

I pondered life in soft moon's glow,
Why do the best shells seem to go?
With every wave, my dreams would purl,
As comets danced, a cosmic whirl.

The tide rolled in with whispering sighs,
Crashing echoes, a lullaby.
I laughed and waved at my sandy friends,
In this warm night, fun never ends.

Coral-Streaked Skies

In a land where coconuts swim,
Bananas wear hats and grin.
Palm trees sway with a cheeky sway,
Sunshine tickles the breeze today.

Seagulls squawk a silly tune,
Dancing under a laughing moon.
Flip-flops gossip on sandy shores,
While crabs play cards and chuckle more.

The waves make jokes in bubbly fits,
Splashing on shores like playful skits.
A dolphin pranks a tourist near,
With a wave and splash, it disappears.

Every sunset beams with delight,
While fireflies waltz in the night.
The whole beach knows it's time to play,
As laughter rings till the break of day.

Lagoon of Laughter

In the lagoon where giggles flow,
Frogs wear ties and put on shows.
Fish tell tales of ancient tides,
And turtles sport their fashionable rides.

With each splash a joke is born,
While flamingos dance on the lawn.
A parrot flaps, a jester bright,
Cracking puns that take flight.

The sunbeam slides on water's face,
While otters race in a bubbly chase.
Bamboo flutes play a hint of cheer,
Bringing all the critters near.

At sunset, everyone's in bliss,
Sharing a laugh, who wouldn't miss?
With humor wrapping the evening tight,
The lagoon whispers sweet goodnight.

Island Serenade

On this isle where fun abounds,
Happiness leaps with joyful bounds.
Bananas, as ukuleles sing,
And mangoes jive in a fruity ring.

The sandmen rise with sandy feet,
Claiming chairs for an idle seat.
With coconut drinks in hand they cheer,
Laughing loudly for all to hear.

The monkeys swing with endless glee,
Stealing hats from tourists nearby.
While palm fronds fan the funny scene,
Creating laughter, bright and keen.

The stars come out with a wink and grin,
As crickets chirp a merry din.
In this paradise of joy and grace,
Each heart dances, each smile a trace.

Driftwood Reverie

Driftwood dreams on the sandy stage,
Crabs in costumes act out a page.
Starfish plot their escape to fame,
In a world where silliness reigns the same.

The tide rolls in with a playful shove,
As seashells giggle with tales of love.
Waves crack jokes, tumbling around,
While joyful echoes blend with the sound.

An octopus juggles shells with flair,
While sunburnt tourists gasp at the air.
Old flip-flops emerge from a sunken boat,
Finding laughter afloat, like a silly note.

As nightfall stamps its playful mark,
Mice in sandals prance through dark.
In dreams, they'll dance till the break of dawn,
A driftwood tale of laughter drawn.

Palm-Studded Horizons

Beneath the palms, we prance around,
Wearing our hats, feeling quite profound.
A monkey stole my drink last night,
Now I'm dodging him with all my might!

The sun is hot, our worries flee,
My flip-flops squeak like a symphony.
A crab danced by, with swagger and flair,
We laughed so hard, we fell from our chairs!

A piña colada in hand, what a thrill,
Dancing like no one, it's quite a skill.
My phone took a dip; oh what a sight,
Now it's swimming too, in pure delight!

With every wave, a giggle bursts,
As seagulls dive, our laughter bursts.
Life here is zany, a whimsical game,
I think I'll stay; I'm never the same.

Warmth of the Waters

Splashing around like fish on dry land,
I rolled off my float with a comical plan.
The sun's relentless, but so is the fun,
Who knew sunscreen could turn me to bun?

A coconut fell, it rolled with a grin,
Hit my friend right in the chin!
We laughed so hard; it echoed so clear,
"Next time, aim for my drink, my dear!"

We built a sandcastle taller than me,
Until a wave came, now it's a sea tree.
A mermaid's laugh? Oh, was that a prank?
Maybe it's just the jug of grape drank!

At sunset, we danced on soft golden grains,
Leading the way to our silly refrains.
Life is a party beneath the big sky,
With every misstep, we just have to fly!

Escape to Eden

In a hammock swaying, I munch on a snack,
While geckos perform a circus act.
A squirrel jumps and steals my hat,
Now I sit under the shade of a cat!

Banana peels scattered, like hidden dreams,
My friends slip and slide, oh how it seems!
A pineapple hat, I proudly wear,
As we gather for pictures, without a spare.

The breeze sings tunes of a lost serenade,
Whisking away all my worries laid.
"Are we lost?" one friend nervously asks,
I reply, "Only if we want snacks!"

Under stars, we make silly wishes,
Hoping for mermaids and sea cucumber dishes.
With every laugh, a new tale unfurls,
In this Eden of giggles, we're capturing swirls.

Solace in Sands

A beach ball flew like a rogue missile,
My friend caught it with a unsinkable chisel.
We tossed it high, with an awkward shout,
And watched it land straight in a crab's route!

The waves crash softly, almost in tune,
While seagulls plot under the sneaky moon.
A towel fight breaks out, it's old school fun,
With salty hair, we'll call it a run!

We raced to the water; our prize was a splash,
But slipped on the wet, and fell with a crash.
"Was that a dance?" a stranger then asked,
We grinned, "Of course, just how we basked!"

As dusk draws near, our giggles remain,
Bringing joy even in light summer rain.
In a world of chaos, we find our free hands,
And create our own magic in the solace of sands.

Paradise's Silent Song

In the hammock, I sway with ease,
Chasing dreams and buzzing bees.
A bird sings in a silly tune,
While crabs dance under the full moon.

Flip-flops flying in the breeze,
Dancing socks among the trees.
One spaghetti noodle, a fishy goll,
Who knew lunch could take a fall?

Watermelon smiles in the sun,
Juicy bites—oh, so much fun!
Sandy toes in a sun-kissed land,
I laugh, I trip; isn't life grand?

The palm trees wave, no hands in sight,
Wishing me good luck tonight.
With sea spray kisses, I'll make jokes,
As the sunset greets the island folks.

Tides of Laughter

Waves crash like a giggling friend,
Tickling toes in a playful blend.
Sunscreen slips on a nose so round,
Not a care, just joy to be found.

Seashells whisper in the sand,
Their secrets flow, like a giant band.
A dolphin leaps—my best dance mate,
With flips and flops, it's not too late!

As kites soar high, the winds do play,
I chase them down, come what may.
With silly hats and drinks so tall,
Who needs a plan when I can sprawl?

The tides bring giggles, waves bring cheer,
Here's to laughter, year after year.
A splash, a yelp, everyone's game,
At this beach, we all feel the same!

The Color of Dawn

Emerald skies as the day awakes,
With sleepy yawns and wiggly shakes.
Bananas wear pajamas, oh so bright,
And coconuts chuckle at morning light.

A monkey swings, it's quite a sight,
Holding a coffee—what a delight!
Bright pink flamingos on the shore,
Uninhibited by their feathered lore.

Mangoes drop like giggling pranks,
While tourists try to avoid the tanks.
With pancakes stacked up to the stars,
We toast to laughter from afar.

In the hush of dawn, jokes take flight,
Filled with wonder, oh what a sight!
With every color, smiles expand,
At this joyful, whimsical land.

Wild Laughter in the Coconut Grove

In the grove, the coconuts chuckle,
As I trip and fall with a silly wuckle.
Palm fronds dance as if in a race,
Swaying to the rhythm of a playful bass.

A swing made of vines takes me for spin,
Laughing hysterically, I land with a grin.
Insects tap dance on my pancake plate,
Sparking giggles I can hardly sate.

Bubbles rise from a drink so sweet,
Feeling bubbly from my head to my feet.
The sun's a giant laughable ball,
Teasing shadows that rise and fall.

With every giggle, spirits soar high,
Coconuts rumble as if to reply.
In this charming grove, we'll never resist,
For wild laughter, we all persist!

Azure Dreams

I packed my bag with flip-flops bright,
And set my sights on skies so light.
The parrot laughed, a cheeky chap,
He stole my sandwich—what a trap!

A coconut fell right on my head,
I danced around, just like I said.
The sun laughed too, a glowing tease,
While I tried hard to swat those bees!

The waves invited, come and play,
But I just tripped, then fell all day.
With sunscreen globs, a sticky mess,
I swam with grace, or was it stress?

As sunset painted skies with cheer,
I toasted llamas with my beer.
With laughter bright and joy so grand,
I found peace in this sunny land.

Swaying Blossoms

In a hammock hung from a palm so grand,
I swung and dreamed, thoughts unplanned.
A bug bit me, it thought it's sleek,
But I waved my arms and gave a squeak!

The flowers giggled with colors bright,
Their secret chatter made me light.
A bee buzzed in with a smile so wide,
I said, "Hey buddy, joining my ride?"

I tried to dance, but stumbled and spun,
The local goat said, "This is fun!"
Together we twirled, a sight to see,
A funny trio, just wild and free.

As night fell down with twinkling lights,
I shared my snacks with the moon in sights.
The stars all winked, in pure delight,
I laughed and cheered, what a silly night!

Mirage of the Moon

Beneath the moon's curious gaze,
I tripped on sand in a goofy daze.
The crabs all clapped, they loved my moves,
While I juggled shells in wave-like grooves.

A mirage danced just out of reach,
I reached for it, while trying to preach.
The shadows chuckled, mocking my aim,
Yet here I was, too wild to tame!

The ocean laughed, a bubbling roar,
As I tried to surf, then fell once more.
With a splat, I made a splashy mark,
In this moonlit fool's paradise, so stark.

But laughter echoed, as stars took flight,
We celebrated mishaps deep into night.
I raised my glass to the tides below,
Cheers to the joy in this funny show!

Sanctuary Beneath the Stars

In my beach chair, I settled down,
With a fruity drink and a silly frown.
The seagulls squawked, they twisted jokes,
I told them tales of oddball folks.

The stars above were twinkling bright,
I waved and winked at each little light.
An octopus joined, said, "Have a seat!"
With eight long arms, he danced to the beat.

We played charades with a fishy twist,
Trying to guess how the dolphins kissed.
A conch shell laughed, it echoed back,
And everyone joined in the fun-filled wrack.

As waves amplified our foolish cheer,
I hugged a palm—no need to steer.
With giggles and joy beneath the sky,
I found my peace, oh me, oh my!

A Symphony of Waves

With ukuleles strumming near,
The seagulls join in without fear.
A beach ball bounces, oh so high,
While sunburnt tourists wave goodbye.

The sand is warm, the drinks are cold,
A sunburn is my badge of bold.
Crabs scuttle sideways, what a sight,
While sunscreen battles, oh, what a fight!

Bikinis slip and flip-flops fly,
As laughter echoes to the sky.
A family picnic gone awry,
With ants that march and pies that cry.

By sunset's glow, we dance and sway,
The waves make music, come what may.
With goofy moves and sandy feet,
This beach life is the ultimate treat!

Sun-Kissed Serenity

My hat is big, my face is red,
Sandwiches brought, but crumbs instead.
A parrot squawks while I just stand,
Trying to draw a perfect hand.

A coconut falls with a loud thump,
While I trip over a beachy lump.
In flip-flops, I'm a comical sight,
An elegant swan turned clumsy kite.

We build a castle – it's a flop,
But oh, how we giggle, can't make it stop.
Seashells exchanged for some goldfish,
I never knew that was my wish!

As stars come out, we huddle tight,
With tales that make the evening bright.
Though sunburnt and tired, smiles bestow,
In this sunny chaos, we steal the show!

Danced by Dunes

Oh, the dunes are steep, I can't decide,
To climb to the top or just take a slide.
The sand is soft, the laughter loud,
As I roll down, feeling so proud.

Kites dance high in the bright blue,
While I try to wrestle with a flip-flop too.
My sunscreen model is looking quite fair,
Though it's splattered more in my hair!

The beachside grill sends scents so fine,
But who thought I'd wear a ketchup line?
Burgers flop and hot dogs tease,
With every bite, I squeal in glee.

At sunset, we twirl, what a grand sight,
With dance moves that are quite a fright!
While grains of sand stick to our toes,
We'll laugh at our mishaps, as everyone knows!

Colors of the Coast

In hues of blue and shades of green,
My beach umbrella stands like a queen.
Sunblock slathered, looking like a ghost,
While I hunt for treasures, that's what I boast!

There's a splash and a scream, a wave in my face,
A fish with my snack? What a wild chase!
With jellyfish bobbing, oh what a show,
My flotation device? A rubber chicken, yo!

Flip-flops off, I'll run for a dip,
But trip on my towel, oh what a trip!
With friends all around, it's laughter we bring,
As we pretend to be mermaids with bling.

The sun sets quickly, but spirits stay high,
With tales of my fall that never run dry.
In shades of pink, the night paints a toast,
To silly adventures, we cherish the most!

Rhapsody of Rainforests

In the jungle, monkeys dance,
Swinging high in their own romance.
Parrots squawk a jaunty tune,
While sloths snooze beneath the moon.

Buzzing bugs in bright array,
Test my patience every day.
Hippo hides in muddy bliss,
"Just five more minutes!" says the miss.

Vines that tangle, leaves that chase,
Every corner holds a face.
Lizards wink with gleeful might,
"Wanna race?" they call with fright.

Amidst the slides of leafy greens,
I lose my way, but never my jeans.
In this realm of fun and play,
Let's laugh and frolic all the day!

Sunrays and Shadows

Beneath the sun, a beach ball bounces,
While sunscreen slips, and laughter announces.
Seagulls steal my sandwich delight,
"Hey! That's mine!" I shout in spite.

Sandcastles lean and start to squish,
A toddler's giggle—a famous dish.
Sunnies on, I strike a pose,
While farmers tan their noses, who knows?

Beach towels fly like kites in the air,
And flip-flops dance without a care.
A crab waves 'hello' with a sidestep twist,
"Join our dance!" I can't resist!

Footprints vanish with every tide,
A race with waves—my new joyride.
In this world of sunny whim,
Life can be silly—just on a whim!

Reflections on Still Waters

Mirrors of nature, ponds so clear,
Frogs sing low for all to hear.
I toss a stone, it skips and flips,
And fish beneath perform their dips.

Dragonflies buzzing, swift as a dart,
Playing tag near the lily's heart.
Turtles bask, with grins abloom,
"Is it hot?" they say, in their cozy room.

A splash! A splash! I can't control,
As I trip and fall; that's my role.
Raccoons giggle from the nearby bush,
"Look at that fellow—what a rush!"

Echoes ripple, laughter's sound,
In this oasis, joy is found.
The world's reflections, every jolt,
Bring humor in nature's hidden vault.

Journey to the Horizon

A ship of dreams on waters wide,
With goats aboard for a silly ride.
They munch the sails, a rogue parade,
As dolphins giggle in the shade.

Maps upside-down and snacks galore,
I can't help but drop my oar.
Captain's hat upon a wig,
"Unfurl the sails!" I dance a jig.

The sun dips low, the sky's ablaze,
While crew members share their silly ways.
"To infinity!" we shout with might,
As the horizon teases goodnight.

Laughter echoes across the blue,
Funny tales of the things we do.
As waves gently rock us altogether,
Every moment, just light as a feather.

A Playground of Palms

Beneath the palms we run and slide,
Where coconuts don't seem to hide.
A monkey swings with quite a flair,
And steals your snack - don't you dare!

We build our castles, oh so grand,
But waves come crashing, isn't that planned?
Sand in our shorts, giggles galore,
Who knew beach days could bring such uproar?

With frisbees flying and laughter loud,
We dance like there's no watching crowd.
The sun may scorch, but spirits rise,
In this playground, we claim the skies!

Memories in the Mist

In fog like soup, we sail away,
Where sea turtles throw a wild ballet.
Laughter echoes through the haze,
As we search for sun on rainy days!

A crab scuttles by, in quite a rush,
Wondering why we all just crush.
We're lost in fun, not in the map,
But who needs paths? Just a sun hat!

With cocktails served in silly cups,
We mix and sip, then spill like pups.
Memories made in this comedic twist,
Raise your glass, it's hard to resist!

Ocean's Embrace

The ocean called, and so we came,
To play some beachy, silly game.
Diving low, we miss the waves,
And end up splashing like a bunch of knaves!

Seagulls swoop, trying to steal,
Our snacks with deftness – what a deal!
We chase them off with goofy shouts,
While laughing at our silly doubts.

In sunburned glory, we lay about,
With ice cream dripping, there's no doubt.
The ocean's hug, a salty brine,
We find our bliss, even when we whine!

The Art of Relaxation

With hammocks swaying, we find our ease,
To gaze at palm trees, if you please.
A lizard's dance, a colorful sight,
Makes us chuckle with pure delight!

Our sunscreen spread shines like a star,
But somehow ends up on my guitar.
Strumming tunes, we laugh and play,
Relaxation – what a humorous way!

As smooth waves lap, we doze and dream,
In our silly hats, we reign supreme.
The art of chill, with friends so dear,
Who knew peace could bring such cheer?

The Stillness of Sunrise

The sun peeks out, a golden grin,
A parrot squawks, let the day begin!
Flip-flops on feet, mischief in sight,
The hammock's too snug, oh what a plight!

Coconuts fall like clumsy friends,
While the crab dances, the laughter never ends.
Sipping on breezes, sipping on tea,
The iguana rolls its eyes at me!

Salty hair, the beach becomes a stage,
Where seagull gossip fuels our rage.
A beach ball flies, oh what a scene,
It hit a sunbather—call it routine!

Sunset comes, we dance with the tide,
The waves embrace, it's our funny stride.
Under starlit skies, we laugh in delight,
With moonlit shenanigans, we own the night!

Journey Through Jade

Green leaves chatter in a breeze so bright,
The monkeys swing, oh what a sight!
Raindrops giggle, they tickle the ground,
And splashes are heard when friends are around.

Lily pads wink, they know how to play,
While frogs croak jokes that carry away.
Navigating paths, where vines like to tease,
Tripping over roots, laughing with ease.

Canoes pass by with a raucous cheer,
As a turtle rolls by, 'I'm a boat, my dear!'
With every turn, nature's slapstick show,
Jade hues shimmer, where hilarity flows.

As night falls, the insects sing loud,
Nature's disco, oh we're so proud!
With every giggle, the stars twinkle bright,
In this green wonderland, all feels just right!

Aromas of the Ocean

The sea breeze whispers secrets of fun,
As salty snacks call for everyone.
Seashells wear hats, they're dressing in style,
While crabs tap dance to the wave's sweet dial.

Skim boards glide like fish on the run,
A seagull swoops, oh how we run!
Chasing the waves, we slip and we zoom,
With laughter echoing, there's no time for gloom.

Fishy faces, as we splash in delight,
A seahorse parade, what a funny sight!
With every wave, mischief is made,
In this sea of smiles, we won't be swayed.

Sunset flavors, with popsicle cheer,
Cracking jokes with a bucket of beer.
As darkness settles, we toast to the night,
With scents of the ocean, our hearts feel light!

Hues of Lush Escape

Palm trees wave in a friendly dance,
Where sunburns and laughter take their chance.
Pineapple hats, oh what a trend,
Holiday mishaps, we can't comprehend!

Mangoes roll like giggly gnomes,
While lizards sneak into our homes.
Tropical drinks bubble with glee,
Each sip we take, we lose our spree.

The sunset drips in colors so wild,
Glowworms twinkle, nature's own child.
As we dodge raindrops that dance on our heads,
We laugh at the chaos—no tears, just threads!

In this land of hues, where joy never tires,
With friends all around, we build our own fires.
Every giggle ignites a new spark,
In this vibrant paradise, we leave our mark!

Cradle of the Tropical Winds

The coconut's a cheeky nut,
It mocks the seagulls' flight,
As waves parade in sundry hues,
And sunbeams spark delight.

Flip-flops dance on sandy feet,
With each misplaced glance and slip,
A crab winks with one big claw,
While sipping juice from a chip.

A parrot squawks a riddle now,
What's green and loves the sun?
I'll tell you later, but for now,
I think I'll take a run!

So here we lounge beneath the sky,
With fruity drinks in hand,
As laughter floats on breezy notes,
Oh, isn't life just grand?

Notes from the Shoreline

A starfish wearing tiny shades,
Looks pretty slick, I'd say,
With beach balls zooming all around,
And kids who laugh and play.

A seagull steals my sandwich quick,
In haste, he takes flight fast,
With toppings flying through the air,
Life's joys have gone awash!

We build a castle, tall and grand,
But watch it start to sink,
The tide's a prankster, just you wait,
It's like it loves to wink.

But laughter echoes on the shore,
As we face another wave,
Life's a feast of silly moments,
In chaos we behave!

When Time Stands Still

With pineapples all dressed in sarongs,
They sway beneath the sun,
While flip-flops giggle on the path,
And every nap's not done.

A hammock swings between two palms,
Where naps are never shy,
I snooze much longer than I planned,
Time laughs when I comply.

The clock just mocks, it spins around,
Insisting I must play,
But then a dolphin jumps just right,
And steals my breath away!

So here I lie beneath the sky,
In sunshine's warm embrace,
The world can wait—I'll just relax,
In this sweet, silly place!

Surfing on Daydreams

In flip-flops, I catch a wave of dreams,
On boards that slide and glide,
I'm a surfing pro in my own mind,
As the tide takes me for a ride.

My dog's my coach, he woofs with glee,
As I wipe out in pure style,
Splashing fish and giggling ducks,
All part of my wild trial!

The ocean swirls in laughter loud,
As seaweed pulls my hair,
I shout, "Help me!", but it just waves,
And bids me to beware!

But as I tumble, thrash, and roll,
I find joy in the spills,
With every wave and wiggly turn,
Life's a ride of thrills!

Celestial Cabana

Beneath the stars, we sip our drinks,
The glowing moon rolls its eyes and winks.
Parrots squawk like they're singing tunes,
While crabs dance like they're in cartoons.

Sunburned noses all around,
We laugh so hard, we nearly drown.
Coconuts won't stay on their tree,
They roll and bounce, wild and free.

Flip flops flying through the air,
Who knew we'd have a foot race there?
Sand in our hair, it's not so bad,
As long as the drinks keep coming, we're glad.

When morning comes, we'll sleep some more,
To dream of crabs and drinks galore!
In our cabana, it's always bright,
With laughter echoing through the night.

Island Echoes

Whispers of waves on a golden shore,
Echoing laughter, who could ask for more?
Seagulls squawk, they want our fries,
Little do they know, it's a food disguise!

In the hammock, swinging high,
One leg up, oh my, oh my!
Sunhats upside down on our heads,
Life's a joke, oh, let it spread!

A barbecue with a fishy tale,
Who cooked the catch? Our boat turned pale!
Tropical fruits, we feast and munch,
Banana peels become our lunch.

As the sun sets with rosy rays,
We throw beach balls like it's a craze.
Dancing shadows in the resort,
Let's keep the fun, never cut short!

Lush Retreat

Palm trees sway like they're in a trance,
We stumble out, hoping for a dance.
Mango juice drips down our chin,
Who knew paradise could be this thin?

Lizards wearing sunglasses—how rude!
They act like they own the whole food.
Sneakers lost in the sand so fine,
Oh well, barefoot is just divine!

A picnic spread that turns into a fight,
With ants in our sandwiches, oh what a sight!
Sunburns ticking like a clock,
But laughter turns the pain to mock.

Late-night stories under the stars,
We argue over who has the best scars.
In our lush hideaway, with friends who cheer,
We sip and chuckle—it's the best time of year!

Secrets of the Lagoon

In a lagoon where frogs wear crowns,
The rumors spread from towns to towns.
Fish float by with quirky grins,
What secrets hide beneath their fins?

Wacky boat rides with giddy screams,
Silly faces turn to memes.
A crab in sunglasses steals our snacks,
While we're busy plotting our next practice hacks.

Splash fights break out and soon it's war,
Dripping laughter spills on the shore.
The mermaids giggle at our best moves,
While we explore our dance grooves.

As day fades into a glowing night,
We gather 'round for tales of fright.
In this lagoon, where laughter's spun,
We've found the charm of endless fun!

Beneath the Canopy

In a jungle of laughter, we sway and twirl,
Where monkeys wear hats and the parrots unfurl.
Palm trees gossip, the breeze tells a joke,
While lizards play cards and the sun starts to choke.

With coconuts bouncing, we sip on our drink,
A cocktail of giggles, don't spill, or you'll stink!
The iguanas all chuckle, they know what's at stake,
An afternoon nap? Or a dance on the lake?

A stray monkey swings by, wearing sunglasses too,
He spins in a circle, and we laugh till we're blue.
The party's in full swing, the fruit's ripe to munch,
Beneath the green canopy, we've got quite the punch!

As the stars start to twinkle, our limbs start to ache,
We'll dream of more laughter, our own little wake.
With dreams of a beach where the fun never ends,
Beneath the canopy, we're all the best friends.

A Voyage to Eden

Set sail on a banana, with laughter as our guide,
We'll cruise past the sunbeams, where dreams collide.
Captain coconut leads us, with a smile so wide,
Seagulls throw confetti, in waves we'll abide.

The tides dance with joy, swapping tales of the sea,
Where jellyfish jiggle and crabs sing with glee.
We'll stop at a reef for a fishy ballet,
Make sure to stay close, or you'll float far away!

With fish wearing top hats and snails in a race,
We laugh as they tumble, in this comical space.
A picnic of seaweed, a feast oh so grand,
As we toast to this voyage, with smoothies on hand!

On this voyage to nowhere, with puns in the breeze,
We'll chart our humor, a map of pure tease.
So let's sail on forever, propelled by the fun,
In our boat made of laughter, we're all number one!

Serene Shores Await

On shores where the laughter washes ashore,
The waves join our giggles, we ask for more.
Sunbathing seagulls compete in a squat,
While starfish compete for the sun's warmest spot.

With flip-flops a-floppin', we dance in the sand,
While crabs throw a conga, isn't life simply grand?
We'll build a sandcastle, but hold onto your hat,
As the tide comes a-charging to ruin our chat!

Pineapple umbrellas in drinks stacked so high,
A seagull dives down, and steals one to fly.
We'll chase after whimsy, let worries be free,
For on these serene shores, it's just you, me, and tea!

As the sun dips low, painting skies with its flare,
We'll laugh at the antics of the beach without care.
With memories made here, and laughter so bright,
Serene shores await us, from morning to night.

The Lure of Distant Seas

Oh, the call of the ocean, with tunes oh so sweet,
Where fish tell tall tales and the turtles repeat.
We'll surf on the waves that ripple with fun,
While octopuses juggle under the sun.

A pirate parrot squawks, "Join me for a spree!"
We'll hunt for lost treasure, a chest filled with glee.
But watch out for jellyfish, they giggle and sting,
In this world of humor, it's quite the wild fling!

Sandcastles rise up, but watch for the waves,
They bubble and chuckle as they crash like brave knaves.
We'll dance with the dolphins, a flip and a splash,
As the sea sings sweet songs in a shimmering flash.

With sunsets that tickle our hearts full of cheer,
We'll toast to our journey, with nothing to fear.
For the lure of these seas brings a grin like no other,
In this ocean of laughter, we'll always discover!

Fluttering Hibiscus

A flower sways, it can't sit still,
In the sun, it laughs, what a thrill!
Bees buzz by, in a silly dance,
Hibiscus giggles, given the chance.

Pineapples wear a crown, quite proud,
Swaying palms join in, oh so loud!
A coconut falls with a plop,
Nature's rhythm, it just won't stop.

Flip-flops flapping in the breeze,
Seagulls squawking, doing as they please.
A parrot squawks a cheeky joke,
While sunbathers giggle, sipping Coke.

Oh, to lounge, a hammock's call,
Falling asleep, I almost sprawl.
But wait, where's my drink? Oh no, I pout,
The beach is fun, but thirst? No doubt!

Echoes of a Coastal Serenity

The ocean waves are quite the singers,
Shells applaud with their tiny fingers.
A crab tiptoes in fancy shoes,
Clicking clacks as it sings the blues.

Seashells gather for a grand ball,
Rhythms echoing, one and all.
A dolphin jumps, quite the comedian,
Spraying water, feels like a median.

Let's not forget the sand, of course,
Rolling in it, such a new discourse.
A friend yells, "Watch out!" with a grin,
Catching a wave, but more like a spin!

A picnic set, but oh dear me!
Ants join the feast, bold as can be.
With laughter echoing through the air,
Coastal charm, nothing can compare!

Sunset Mirage

Colors splash like paint on the sky,
A parrot named Larry, oh my, oh my!
He struts around in a dazzling hue,
But complains that his dinner's overdue!

Palm trees dance in a breezy sway,
Whispering secrets at close of day.
A couple stumbles in love's embrace,
But trips on a flip-flop, what a disgrace!

Picnic tables dressed up in crumbs,
Squirrel guests invite their whole clans of chums.
A sunset toast spills over the edge,
A toast to mishaps, we all pledge!

As the day ends, we burst into song,
Laughing at where we all went wrong.
With a sunset glow, our spirits align,
In this mirage, everything's fine!

Sands of Time

The hourglass spills sandy grains,
Tickling toes, oh the fun, it remains!
Time flies by when you're making pies,
Cardboard surfboards under clear skies.

A sandcastle tall, but the tide has a plan,
"Big waves are coming!" we shout with a pan.
Laughter erupts as it washes away,
We build it again, come what may!

Seagulls swoop in for a sandwich bite,
Mischief in their eyes, taking flight.
The clock might tick, but who cares?
Grains of joy are found in hair!

So let's pretend we don't have a care,
Time spent in sun is beyond compare.
In each moment, a giggle divine,
Living our days, through the sands of time!

Salt of the Soul

Lime slices jump in my coconut drink,
Waves lapping shores, time to rethink.
A lazy dog on a sun-soaked chair,
Chasing dreams without a single care.

Frolicking dolphins in synchronized sway,
Picking up jokes as they play all day.
A fishy friend winks, scales all aglow,
This underwater party? Quite the show!

Salt in the air, a seasoning's delight,
Laughter bubbles up into the night.
As stars twinkle brightly from the skies,
Even the moon can't help but rise.

From waves to drinks, every detail matters,
Tidal splashes and silly patters.
The heart's a beach, where laughter rolls,
In this cheery realm, we're the salt of our souls!

Enchanted by the Breeze

A coconut fell, a light-hearted thud,
As seagulls squawked in playful flood.
Palm trees swayed with a cheeky grin,
Inviting all to join in the spin.

The sun wore shades, quite the cool dude,
While flip-flops danced in an artful mood.
Mangoes juggled like circus beans,
Amidst laughter, where joy intervenes.

Chasing crabs on the sandy shore,
They scampered away as they heard us roar.
With every splash and every cheer,
A silly escape became quite clear.

So here's to breezes, both mild and wild,
Making us feel like a carefree child.
With sunshine smiles and silly glee,
We found our joy, as wild as the sea.

Paradise Found in Paradise Lost

In search of bliss, we lost our way,
And found a llama at the beach chair stray.
With sunglasses on, he sipped his drink,
A sight so strange, it made us think.

The map was upside down, what a site!
Instead of gold, we found pure delight.
Skimpy shorts and a wayward hat,
As we lounged, we embraced the chat.

All my worries washed away at last,
With every giggle, a memory cast.
In flip-flopping chaos, we found the glee,
Who knew plight could be so carefree?

So here's to losing our way in the sun,
Finding paradise while having fun.
With irony's wink, we laugh and toast,
To the whims that we cherish the most.

Dance of the Waves

The waves decided it's time to play,
Bouncing up high in a bubbly way.
Seashells clapped with their painted souls,
As surfboards twirled like mischievous shoals.

A crab on a board, what a sight to see!
Dancing and prancing, embodying glee.
The ocean chuckled, a fit of mirth,
As sandcastles trembled, giving birth.

Splashing and crashing, the rhythm grew,
With seaweed wigs, a hilarious crew.
Fish twirled around, swaying their fins,
As laughter swelled, and mischief begins.

So join the frolic, no need to hide,
In the dance of the waves, we take our ride.
With every dip and every dive,
We discover together, the joy to thrive.

Secrets of the Coral Reef

Beneath the waves, a whispering plot,
Where fish wear hats, oh, what a lot!
Corals giggle, in colors they flaunt,
With anemone clowns performing their jaunt.

Sea turtles drift with a carefree grace,
While octopuses paint their own space.
Secrets bubble in this underwater dance,
As the jellyfish sway in a trance.

With a wink and a swish, the stingrays glide,
A parade of colors is hard to hide.
The ocean chuckles, revealing its best,
In the curious depths, we find our quest.

So dive into giggles and splash with zest,
Discovering wonders that never rest.
In the charm of the reef, hilarity thrives,
Where nature's secrets bring laughter alive.

www.ingramcontent.com/pod-product-compliance
Lightning Source LLC
Chambersburg PA
CBHW072130070526
44585CB00016B/1607